DATE DUE   CHILDREN ROOM

ST. VALENTINE'S DAY

A Crowell Holiday Book

St. Valentine's Day

BY CLYDE ROBERT BULLA

Illustrations by Valenti Angelo

THOMAS Y. CROWELL COMPANY

NEW YORK

Crowell Holiday Books

Edited by Susan Bartlett Weber

ST. VALENTINE'S DAY

PASSOVER

ARBOR DAY

FLAG DAY

MOTHER'S DAY

1 2 3 4 5 6 7 8 9 10

ST. VALENTINE'S DAY

St. Valentine's Day is one of our oldest holidays. It was old before there was a land called America.

Thousands of years ago this holiday was celebrated in Rome. But in those times the Romans did not call it St. Valentine's Day. Their name for it was Lupercalia.

Lupercalia means "feasts of Lupercus."

The Romans believed that a god named Lupercus helped protect them from wolves. He was an important god to the people, because wolves were a great danger in Rome. These fierce, hungry animals lived in the

woods that covered most of the land. They carried off the farmers' sheep and goats. They were so bold that even the farmers and their families were not always safe.

Each year, in the middle of February, the Romans had feasts to honor their god, Lupercus. They gave thanks to him for helping protect them from the wolves.

At the time of Lupercalia, the people feasted and danced and played games. When the young men wanted partners for the dances and games, they drew the names

of girls out of a bowl. These girls would be their partners.

Often they became the young men's sweethearts, too.

For hundreds of years the people celebrated Lupercalia. Then the Christian reli-
gion came to Rome.

The Romans no longer believed in such gods as Lupercus. But Lupercalia was a happy time. The people did not want to give it up.

So they kept their holiday in the middle of February. But now, at the feasts, they honored a man of the church. He was a saint who had died in Rome on February 14. His name was St. Valentine.

St. Valentine lived so long ago that we do not know much about him. We do know that he lived and died in Rome.

February 14 became known as St. Valentine's Day.

As years went by, celebrations of St. Valentine's Day spread to France and England.

Some of these celebrations were like those of the Romans. There were still feasts and games and dancing. A young man still chose his partner by drawing a girl's name out of a bowl.

In England it was believed that birds chose
their mates on February 14, and so people
looked on this as a good day for choosing
their sweethearts.

When a man chose his sweetheart on St. Valentine's Day, he called her his valentine.

On St. Valentine's Day, sweethearts wrote letters to one another. Their letters were called valentines, too.

At first these were only a few words.

Then people began to draw pictures on their letters.

Someone might draw a picture of a heart and write beneath it, "I give you my heart."

I give you my heart

Or someone might draw flowers and lace
on a valentine just to make it beautiful.

Some wrote verses on their valentines. Some gave gifts to their sweethearts, too. Favorite gifts were candy and cakes, flowers, and jewels.

Hundreds of years ago, in England, children dressed as grownups on St. Valentine's Day. Then they went from house to house, singing valentine songs. Here is one of the songs they sang:

"Good morning to you, valentine.
Curl your locks as I do mine—
Two before and three behind.
Good morning to you, valentine."

When the English came to America, they brought St. Valentine's Day with them. It is still one of our favorite holidays.

Once only sweethearts gave valentines to one another. Now we all give valentines to people we like.

We give them at home and at school. We take them to neighbors. We send them in the mail.

Some have verses like this:

*"Days will all be fair and fine,
As long as you're my valentine."*

Other valentine verses are jokes, like this
one from a girl to a boy:

"*Roses are red,*
Violets are blue.
I pity the girl
Who marries you."

In stores we can buy many different kinds of valentines. Or we can make our own, with scissors and paper and colors and paste.

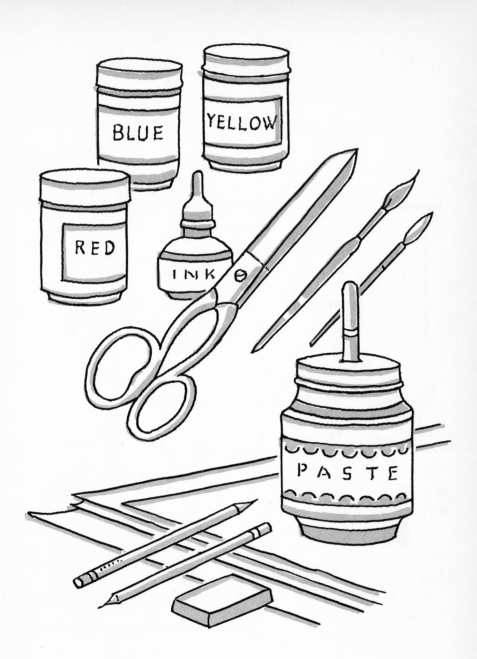

Sometimes we have parties to celebrate February 14. We may give one another valentines and have good things to eat. We may

dance and play games. Boys and girls may
choose partners.

Some of our Valentine parties today may be a little like the feasts on St. Valentine's Day in Rome a long time ago.

ABOUT THE AUTHOR

Clyde Robert Bulla was born near King City, Missouri. He received his early education in a one-room schoolhouse, where he began writing stories and songs. He finished his first book shortly after graduation from high school and then went to work on a newspaper as a columnist and a typesetter.

He continued to write, and his books for children became so successful that he was able to satisfy his desire to travel through the United States, Mexico, Hawaii, and Europe. He lives in Los Angeles, California.

In 1962, Mr. Bulla received the first award of the Southern California Council on Children's Literature for distinguished contributions to the field of children's literature. He has written many stories for young readers.

ABOUT THE ARTIST

Valenti Angelo's earliest memories are of a small village in the Little Alps of northern Italy. He was inspired to paint at a very young age, and this urge continued when his family came to America and moved first to New York City and then to California. Life in crowded tenement areas was as picturesque to Mr. Angelo as the wonders of the countryside. Although he sometimes had to work hard as a laborer, he always found time to visit libraries and museums, where he gained his real education.

After much struggle he found a job in the field of art and began to devote all his time to painting and writing. Mr. Angelo has illustrated more than two hundred books and has written more than a dozen stories for children. He lives near New York City and continues to find new subjects to write about and new subjects to paint.